IN MY OWN WORDS

A guided journal on life, lessons and legacy

Created by **Natalie B. Dean**

In My Own Words: A guided journal on life, lessons and legacy
Copyright © 2022 by Natalie B. Dean.

Books may be purchased in bulk quantity and/or special sales by contacting the publisher.

Published by Mynd Matters Publishing
715 Peachtree Street NE
Suites 100 & 200
Atlanta, GA 30308
www.myndmatterspublishing.com

ISBN: 978-1-957092-40-9

Designed by Kion Lofton, Purpuhs, LLC
Reviewed by Lauren N. Smith, M.Ed. NBC-HWC, BCC
Edited by Tawni Fears, The Tawni Logues, LLC

For information visit nataliebdean.com.

FIRST EDITION

The concept for this journal honors
all the ancestors whose stories were
lost, forgotten or untold.

CONTENTS

BEFORE YOU BEGIN...

May this journal guide you as you recount your life, in your own words, for the benefit of future generations. Significant intention and consideration were put into developing the prompts and design of each page. In addition, the content has been reviewed by a trained psychologist and life coach for appropriateness and sensitivity to ensure your ease and comfort when answering each prompt. However, if a question is triggering or causes any degree of discomfort, feel free to skip it and move to the next prompt. You decide how much you are willing to share.

While I aimed to be as inclusive as possible, should there be any titles, roles, or other identifying terms that don't align with you, relabel them so this journal is most true to who you are.

IN THE
BEGINNING

About me

Full Name

Birthdate

Place of Birth

Nationality

Parents' Names, Birthdates and Birthplaces

Do/Did you have any siblings?
If so, name them in order of oldest to youngest.

My Family Tree

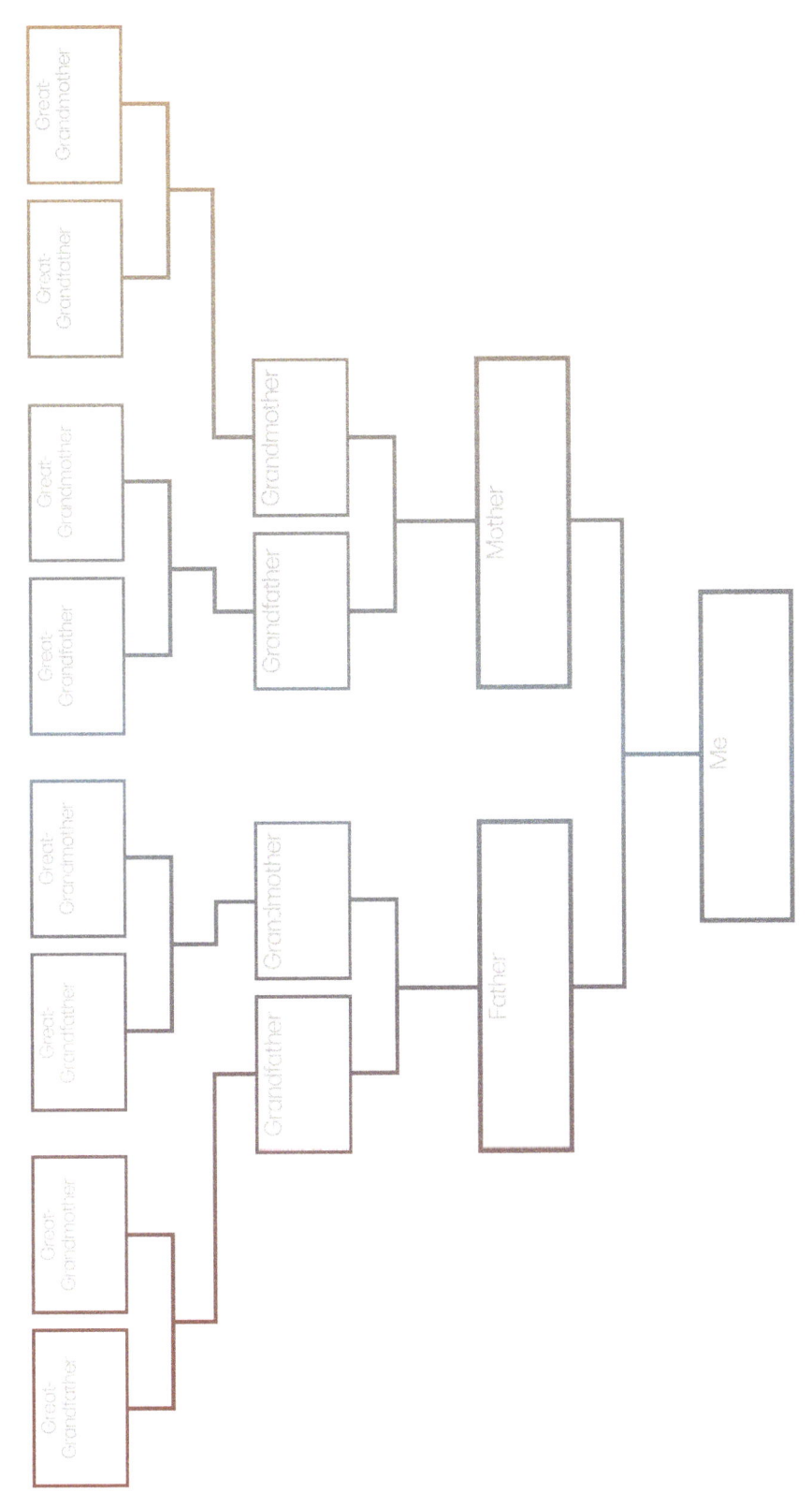

Share what you know about your parents and/or grandparents and how they met.

What were you told about the events surrounding your birth?

Does your name have a special meaning or story behind why it was given to you?

Do you have a family nickname? If so, how did you get the name?

How would you describe your parents/guardians?

Tell me about your relationship with your parents/guardians.

In what ways did you want to be like them?

In what ways did you want to be different from them?

What words would you use to describe your childhood?

-
-
-
-
-
-
-
-
-

What would you have liked to see your parents/guardians do differently when raising you?

What are some skills or life hacks passed down from your elders?

What words of wisdom did the elders in your life impart?

How did others describe you as a child?

Was their description accurate?

How would you describe yourself as a child?

What were your favorite snacks or meals growing up, and who prepared them best?

What are the earliest or most vivid memories of your childhood?

How did your neighborhood or city/town shape who you are?

Tell me about a fond/funny memory with your childhood best friend.

FAVES
As a child, what was your favorite:

Book

Toy/Game

Song

Movie

Dance Move

What did you want to be when you grew up?

Did you become that? If not, what changed your course?

What I know now about this time in my life that I did not know or appreciate then is...

THE
WONDER
YEARS

What type of student were you?

What was it about your favorite subject(s) in school that made you like/love it?

What was it about your least favorite subject(s) in school that made you dislike/not love it?

What extracurricular activities were you involved in at school or in your neighborhood?

Did you experience bullying (as the perpetrator, the victim, or bystander)?

If so, did this affect your time in school? How?

Did your parents/guardians think your friends were a good or bad influence?

How did your teachers describe you?

Was their description accurate?

Who were your closest friends?

-
-
-
-
-
-
-
-

What did you and your friends do for fun?

-
-
-
-
-
-
-
-

Did you ever cut class or skip school? If so, what did you do? Did you get caught?

Who is/was your celebrity crush and why?

Were you a natural-born leader or did you tend to follow the crowd?

What issues were most important to you during your teenage years?

-
-
-
-
-
-
-
-

-
-
-
-
-
-
-
-

Did you advocate on behalf of others or for a specific cause?

What are some major events you experienced during:

Elementary School (year:).

Middle School (year:).

High School (year:).

What did you have the most fun doing when you were in:

Elementary School (year:).

Middle School (year:).

High School (year:).

Share the story of your first:

Crush/Love

Job

Fight

Heartbreak or Loss

What was the first concert you attended and/or movie you went to see?

What were some of your favorite songs or television shows from this era?

Which teacher, mentor, or friend had the biggest impact on you? Why?

Did you have a class superlative (i.e., Most Likely to Succeed)?

If not, what should it have been?

List all the schools you attended, where and when.

Did you attend college? Why or why not?

What were some of the deciding factors when picking a college or vocation?

What events or memories stick out most to you about your early twenties?

Did you make any friends during this time that you are still friends with today?

If so, how did you sustain these relationships over the years?

In what ways did this time in your life shape who you are today?

What I know now about this time in my life that I did not know or appreciate then is...

WINS & LESSONS

What are some inspiring or challenging things you learned about yourself over the years?

What is the most important thing you have had to learn about:

Love

Work

Marriage (if applicable)

Parenting (if applicable)

Friendships

Money

Religion

Politics

Sex and/or Sexuality

Gender Roles

What piece(s) of advice has stuck with you over the years? Who advised you (if you can remember)?

What are three things not worth losing sleep over for you?

1

2

3

What are some of the pros and cons of getting older?

Pros

-
-
-
-
-
-
-
-

Cons

-
-
-
-
-
-
-
-

What are some of the biggest mistakes you've made and what did you learn from them?

What are some things you wish you had done when you were:

Younger

Single

Childless (if applicable)

Scared

First Married (if applicable)

What is a piece of advice you wish you had taken?

Why did you not take it at the time?

How can you take that advice into account at this point in your life?

What are some things you would like to try for the first time?

What is something you cannot help but laugh at yourself for doing?

What are some big goals you have achieved in your life so far?

What is the achievement you are most proud of and why?

Have you won any awards or received any honors?
List them below.

The most courageous thing I have done in life was...

FAVES

List the books, religious passages, proverbs, or quotes you enjoy most.

-
-
-
-
-
-
-
-
-
-
-
-
-
-
-

How do you determine whether or not to keep a:

Friend

Job

Partner/Relationship

When did you start working full time?

Where did you work?

What was your role?

Have you ever been fired from a job or had a negative experience at work?

If so, what happened, and how did you recover?

What advice do you have for dealing with horrible bosses or difficult coworkers?

Do you have any colleagues that became true friends?

If so, how or why did the relationship evolve?

What advice do you have on interviewing for a job or negotiating a promotion/raise?

What is some of the best and worst career advice you have ever received?

What job have you held the longest?

What is/was your title and responsibility?

What did you enjoy about the job?

What did you not enjoy about the job?

What I know now about this time in my life that I did not know or appreciate then is...

LOVE &
LEGACY

In what ways do you practice self-love?

Did you ever struggle with loving yourself?

If so, how did you overcome it?

What do you love most about yourself?

How did your love of self, or lack thereof, impact your romantic relationships?

What are three important characteristics to look for in a romantic partner?

1.

2.

3.

What are some red flags to beware of in a relationship?

How did you meet your spouse or partner (if applicable)?

What attracted you to them?

Did you have a wedding?

What was most memorable about the day?

WEDDING DAY

Date

Flower Girl

Maid & Matron of Honor

Bridesmaids

Best Man

Groomsmen

Ring bearer

If you are still together (or if you were separated by death), what sustains you as a couple?

What were some of the biggest challenges in the relationship and how did you overcome them?

If you are separated or divorced, what were the pros and cons of the relationship while you were together?

Did you remarry or re-partner?

If so, how did you find love again, and what have you learned from this relationship?

What are you most proud of when it comes to your loving relationships?

What examples of love or relationship goals did you use as a guide?

What was your reaction to finding out you'd be a parent/
guardian/aunt/uncle for the first time?

In what ways did you prepare to be a parent/guardian/aunt/uncle?

What is your parenting style?

What experiences shaped your parenting style?

What experiences were you not prepared for with parenting?

What advice would you give to those in any stage of parenthood?

What family traditions did you pass on to your child(ren)?

What family cycles did you end?

What do you enjoy most about being a parent/guardian/ aunt/uncle?

Some things I wish I would have done differently when raising my child(ren) were:

Some things I am proud I did when raising my child(ren) were:

What was one of the hardest moments of being a parent/guardian/aunt/uncle?

As a parent/guardian/aunt/uncle, I am most proud of:

What I know now about this time in my life that I did not know or appreciate then is...

LIFE
REFLECTIONS

Recount an important decision you have made, completely leaning on faith.

What are the three happiest moments in your life so far?

1.

2.

3.

Share a list of 10 things you're grateful for today.

1.

2.

3.

4.

5.

6.

7.

8.

9.

10.

Are there any dreams you still want to come true?

My guilty pleasures are:

What brings you to tears?

What makes you laugh hysterically?

Share a memorable birthday.

What worries you the most?

What gives you hope?

My dos and don'ts of life are:

Dos   Don'ts

What are some of the most memorable events you have attended?

If you can, include the date and location

What is something you never thought you would experience in your lifetime but did?

What is your favorite song, and what memory or feeling does it evoke?

What was your favorite decade and why?

What are some things you have feared in life?

Have you overcome those fears? If so, how? If not, how have they held you back?

What are your political beliefs?
What or who shaped them?

My unpopular opinions are:

Share your most embarrassing moment.

How did you recover?

Questions I have always pondered the answers to are:

What songs would be included on the soundtrack of your life?

Are there any relationships that currently need mending?

If so, what would it take to mend them?

Any trade secrets (beauty tips, recipes, etc.) you wish to pass down?

Share them below.

How do you manage uncomfortable feelings?

Share a time when you had to have a difficult conversation.

What was the result, and how did it make you feel?

What brings you joy?

How would you like to be remembered?

What I know now about life, lessons and legacy that I haven't already shared is...

Should you need more space, use these pages to continue writing.